This Dua Book Belongs To

Table Of Contents

DUA BEFORE SLEEP:

اللَّهُمَّ بِاسْمِكَ أَمُوتُ وَأَحْيَا

'Allahumma Bismika Amutu Wa Ahya'

(O Allah, with Your name I die and live)

DUA AFTER WAKING UP :

اَلْحَمْدُ لِلَّهِ الَّذِي أَحْيَانَا بَعْدَ مَا أَمَاتَنَا وَإِلَيْهِ النُّشُورُ

Alhamdu lillahil-lathee ahyana baAAda ma amatana wa-ilayhin-nushoor.

(All praise is for Allah who gave us life after having taken it from us and unto Him is the resurrection.)

DUA AFTER HAVING A GOOD DREAM :

ٱلْحَمْدُ لِلَّٰ

"Alhamdulillah"

Praise Be To Allah

DUA AFTER HAVING A BAD DREAM :

أَعُوذُ بِاللهِ مِنَ الشَّيْطَانِ الرَّجِيمِ

Awoodhu billaahi minash-shaytaanir-rajeem

"I seek refuge in Allah from the outcast Shaitan".

Dua Before Entering The Bathroom:

اللَّهُمَّ إِنِّي أَعُوذُ بِكَ مِنَ الْخُبْثِ وَالْخَبَائِثِ

Allaahumma 'innee 'a'oothu bika minal-khubthi walkhabaa'ith.

"O Allah. I seek refuge in You from the male female evil and Jinns".

Dua After Leaving The Bathroom:

غُفْرَانَكَ

ghufraanak

I ask You (Allah) for forgiveness.

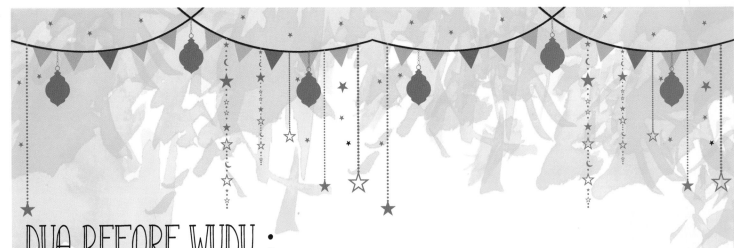

DUA BEFORE WUDU :

ابِسْمِ الله

Bismillaah

In the name of Allah.

DUA AFTER WUDU :

سُبْحَانَكَ اللَّهُمَّ وَبِحَمْدِكَ أَشْهَدُ أَنْ لَا إِلَهَ إِلَّا أَنْتَ أَسْتَغْفِرُكَ وَأَتُوبُ إِلَيْكَ

Subhaanak-allaahumma wa bihamdika ash-hadu an laa ilaha illaa anta astaghfiruka wa atoobu ilayk.

"How far from imperfections You are O Allah, and I praise You, I bear witness that none has the right to be worshipped except You, I seek Your forgiveness and turn in repentance to You."

Dua when putting on a garment :

الْحَمْدُ لِلّهِ الَّذِي كَسَانِي هَذَا الثَّوْبَ وَرَزَقَنِيهِ مِنْ غَيْرِ حَوْلٍ مِنِّي وَلَا قُوَّةٍ

Alḥamdu lillaahil-ladhee kasaanee haadhath-thawba wa razaqaneehi min ghayri ḥawlin minnee wa laa quwwah

All Praise is for Allah who has clothed me with this garment and provided it for me, with no power nor might from myself.

Dua when putting on a new garment :

اللَّهُمَّ لَكَ الْحَمْدُ أَنْتَ كَسَوْتَنِيهِ ، أَسْأَلُكَ مِنْ خَيْرِهِ وَخَيْرِ مَا صُنِعَ لَهُ ، وَأَعُوذُ بِكَ مِنْ شَرِّهِ وَشَرِّ مَا صُنِعَ لَهُ

Allaahumma lakal-ḥamdu anta kasawtaneehi, as'aluka min khayrihi wa khayri maa ṣuni'a lahu, wa 'a'oodhu bika min sharrihi wa sharri maa ṣuni'a lah

O Allah, to You belongs all praise, You have clothed me with it (i.e. the garment), I ask You for the good of it and the good for which it was made, and I seek refuge with You from the evil of it and the evil for which it was made.

Dua said to someone seen wearing a new garment :

اِلْبَسْ جَدِيدًا وَعِشْ حَمِيدًا وَمُتْ شَهِيدًا

Ilbas jadeedan, wa'ish hameedan, wa mut shaheedan

Wear anew, live commendably and die a shaheed.

Dua before undressing:

بِسْمِ الله

Bismillaah

In the name of Allah.

Dua When looking into the mirror:

اللَّهُمَّ أَنْتَ حَسَّنْتَ خَلْقِي فَحَسِّنْ خُلُقِي

Allahumma antha hasantha khalqi fa hasintha khulqi

O Allah, just as You have made my external features beautiful, make my character beautiful as well.

Dua For Parents:

رَبِّ ارْحَمْهُمَا كَمَا رَبَّيَانِي صَغِيرً

Rabb-irhamhumaa kamaa rabbayaanee Sagheeraa

"My Lord, have mercy upon them as they brought me up [when I was] a child."

Dua To Recite Morning & Evening:

بِسْمِ اللهِ الَّذِي لَا يَضُرُّ مَعَ اسْمِهِ شَيْءٌ فِي الْأَرْضِ وَلَا فِي السَّمَاءِ وَهُوَ السَّمِيعُ الْعَلِيمُ

Bismillaahil-ladhee laa yadurru ma'asmihi shay'un fil-ardi wa laa fis-samaa'i wa huwas-samee'-ul-'aleem (x3)

The messenger of Allah (may the peace and blessings of Allah be upon him) said: 'He who says in the morning and the evening of each day Nothing shall harm him'

"In the name of Allah, by whose name nothing can cause harm neither on earth nor in the heaven and He is The All-Hearing, The All-Knowing." (three times)

سُبْحَانَ اللهِ وَبِحَمْدِهِ

Subhaan-allaahi wa bihamdihi (100 times)

How far from imperfections Allah is and I praise Him." (one hundred times)

The messenger of Allah said: whoever says in the morning and the evening :

None will come on the day of judgement with something better, except for someone who said the same.

*[And in another narration] His/her sins will be forgiven, even if they were like the foam of the sea.

Dua For Knowledge:

رَبِّ زِدْنِي عِلْماً

Rabbi Jidni Ilma

"My lord, increase me in my knowledge"

Dua for protection from illness and disease(covid 19):

اللَّهُمَّ إِنِّي أَعُوذُ بِكَ مِنَ الْبَرَصِ، وَالْجُنُونِ، وَالْجُذَامِ، وَمِنْ سَيِّئِ الأَسْقَامِ

Allah humma inni a'udhu bika minal-barasi, wal-jununi, wal-judhaami, wa min sayyi'il-asqaami

"O Allah, I seek refuge in You from leprosy, insanity, elephantiasis, and the worst of diseases."

Dua before eating and drinking:

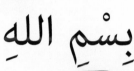

Bismillaah

"In the name of Allah."

Dua made if you forgot to say "Bismillah" before eating:

بِسْمِ اللهِ فِي أَوَّلِهِ وَآخِرِهِ

Bismillaahi fee awwalihi wa aakhirihi

"In the name of Allah in it's beginning and end."

Dua after drinking milk:

اللَّهُمَّ بَارِكْ لَنَا فِيهِ وَزِدْنَا مِنْهُ

Allaahumma baarik lanaa feehi wa zidnaa minh

"O Allah, bless it for us and give us more of it."

Dua made after eating:

الْحَمْدُ لِلَّهِ الَّذِى أَطْعَمَنَا وَسَقَانَا وَجَعَلَنَا مِنَ الْمُسْلِمِين

"Alhamdulillah hillazi at'amanaa wa saqaanaa wa ja'alana minal Muslimiin"

All praises are due to Allah who has provided us with food and drink and made us Muslims.

Dua Made When Entering The Masjid:

السَّلامُ عَلَى رَسُولِ اللهِ ، اللَّهُمَّ افْتَحْ لِي أَبْوَابَ رَحْمَتِكَ

As-salaamu 'alaa rasoolillaah, allaahum-maf-ta' lee abwaaba rahmatik

Peace be upon the Messenger of Allah. O Allah, Open for me the gates of Your Mercy.

Dua Made When Leaving The Masjid:

السَّلامُ عَلَى رَسُولِ اللهِ، اللَّهُمَّ إِنِّي أَسْأَلُكَ مِنْ فَضْلِكَ

As-salaamu 'alaa rasool-lil-laah, allaa-hum-ma innee as'aluka min fad-lik

Peace be upon the Messenger of Allah. O Allah, I ask You from Your favour.

Dua When leaving Home:

.بِسْمِ اللهِ تَوَكَّلْتُ عَلَى اللهِ، وَلاَ حَوْلَ وَلاَ قُوَّةَ إِلاَّ بِاللهِ

Bismil-lah, tawakkaltu AAalal-lah, wala hawla wala quwwata illa billah.

In the name of Allah, I place my trust in Allah, and there is no might nor power except with Allah.

Dua When Entering The House:

Islamic Greeting

ٱلسَّلَامُ عَلَيْكُمْ

As-salāmu alaykum

"Peace be upon you"

Reply To The Islamic Greeting

وَعَلَيْكُمُ ٱلسَّلَامُ

wa alaykumu s-salām

"And peace be upon you, too."

Dua While Biding Good Bye:

أَسْتَوْدِعُ اللَّهَ دِيْنَكَ وَأَمَانتَكَ، وَخَواتِيْمَ عَمَلِكَ

'Astawdi' laha deenaka wa'amanataka wa khatima amaleek.'

(I entrust to Allah your belief, what you are responsible for, and your final deeds.)

Dua Made When Riding In A Vehicle:

سُبْحَانَ الَّذِي سَخَّرَ لَنَا هَذَا وَمَا كُنَّا لَهُ مُقْرِنِينَ وَإِنَّا إِلَى رَبِّنَا لَمُنْقَلِبُونَ.

Subhana-alladhi sakh-khara la-na hadha wa ma kunna la-hu muqrinin.
Wa inna ila Rabbi-na la munqalibun.

Glory unto Him Who created this transportation, for us, though we were unable to create it on our own. And unto our Lord we shall return.

Dua Made When Going High And Low During Ajourney

When Going High Say:

سبحان الله

SubhaanAllah

Glory Is To Allah

When Going Low Say:

الله أكبر

Allahu Akbar

Allah Is The Greatest

Dua Made When Angry:

أَعُوذُ بِاللهِ مِنَ الشَّيْطَانِ الرَّجِيمِ

Awoodhu billaahi minash-shaytaanir-rajeem

"I seek refuge in Allah from the outcast Shaitan".

Dua Made When Happy:

الْحَمْدُ لِلَّهِ الَّذِي بِنِعْمَتِهِ تَتِمُّ الصَّالِحَاتُ

Alhamdulillahil lathee bi ni'matihi tatimmus saalihaat

All praise and thanks are only for Allah, the One who, by His blessing and favor, perfected good-ness/good works are accomplished.

Dua Made When Sad:

الْحَمْدُ لِلَّهِ عَلَى كُلِّ حَالٍ

Alhamdulillah Ala Kulli Haal

All praise and thanks are only for Allah in all circumstances.

Dua Made When We Do Something Bad:

أَسْتَغْفِرُ ٱللَّهَ

Astaġfiru -llāh

I seek forgiveness in Allah

Dua When Sneezing And It's Reply

Person1 (sneezes) and says:

اَلْحَمْدُ لله

Al-ḥamdu lillāh

Praise be to Allah

When you witness this you should say:

يرحمك الله

Yarhamuk Allah

May Allah have Mercy on you

Person1:

يَهْدِيكُمُ اللَّهُ وَيُصْلِحُ بَالَكُمْ

Yahdeekumul-lahu wa yuslihu balakum

May Allah guide you and set your affairs in order

Dua When Entering The Market

لَا إِلَهَ إِلَّا اللهُ وَحْدَهُ لَا شَرِيكَ لَهُ ، لَهُ الْمُلْكُ وَلَهُ الْحَمْدُ ، يُحْيِي وَيُمِيتُ وَهُوَ حَيٌّ لَا يَمُوتُ ، بِيَدِهِ الْخَيْرُ وَهُوَ عَلَى كُلِّ شَيْءٍ قَدِيرٌ

laa ilaaha ill-allaahu wahdahu laa shareeka lah, lah-ul-mulku wa lahul-hamdu, yuhyee wa yumeetu wa huwa hayun laa yamootu, bi yadi-hil-khayru, wa huwa 'alaa kulli shay'in qadeer.

"None has the right to be worshipped except Allah, alone, without partner, to Him belongs all sovereignty and praise. He gives life and causes death, and He is living and does not die. In His hand is all good and He Omnipotent over all things."

Dua For Rain:

اللَّهُمَّ أَغِثْنَا ، اللَّهُمَّ أَغِثْنَا ، اللَّهُمَّ أَغِثْنَا

Allaahumma aghith-naa, allaahumma aghith-naa, allaahumma aghith-naa

O Allah, relieve us, O Allah, relieve us, O Allah, relieve us.

Dua When It's Raining:

اللَّهُمَّ صَيِّبًا نَافِعًا

Allaahumma sayyiban naafi"aa

O Allah, may it be a beneficial rain.

Dua After The Rain Has Fallen:

مُطِرْنَا بِفَضْلِ اللهِ وَرَحْمَتِه

mutirnaa bi fadlil-laahi wa rahmatih

We have been given rain by the grace and mercy of Allah.

Dua for the rain to stop:

اللَّهُمَّ حَوْلَنَا وَلَا عَلَيْنَا ، اللَّهُمَّ عَلَى الآكَامِ وَالظِّرَابِ ، وَبُطُونِ الأَوْدِيَةِ ، وَمَنَابِتِ الشَّجَرِ

allaahumma hawlanaa wa laa 'alaynaa, allaahumma "alal-aakaami waz-ziraabi, wa butoonil-awdiyati, wa ma-naabitish-shajar

O Allah, let the rain fall around us and not upon us, O Allah, (let it fall) on the pastures, hills, valleys and the roots of trees.

Dua upon hearing thunder:

سُبْحَانَ الَّذِي يُسَبِّحُ الرَّعْدُ بِحَمْدِهِ ، وَالْمَلائِكَةُ مِنْ خِيفَتِهِ

subhaan-alladhee yusabbih-ur-ra'du bi hamdihi, wal-ma-laa'ikatu min kheefatih

"How far from imperfections He is, (The One) Whom the thunder declares His perfection with His praise, as do the angels out of fear of Him."

Dua when visiting the sick:

لَا بَأْسَ طَهُورٌ إِنْ شَاءَ اللهُ

laa ba'sa tahoorun in shaa'-alla

"No harm, may it (the sickness) be a purification (for you), if Allah wills."

Dua when sighting the new moon:

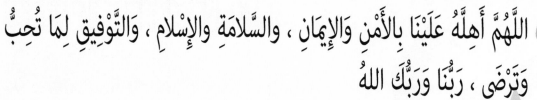

اللَّهُمَّ أَهِلَّهُ عَلَيْنَا بِالأَمْنِ وَالإِيمَانِ ، وَالسَّلَامَةِ وَالإِسْلَامِ ، وَالتَّوْفِيقِ لِمَا تُحِبُّ وَتَرْضَى ، رَبُّنَا وَرَبُّكَ اللهُ

allaahumma ahillahu 'alaynaa bil-amni wal-eemaani, was-sa-laamati wal-islaami, wat-tawfeeqi limaa tuhibbu watardaa, rabunaa wa rabbuk-allaahu

"O Allah, let this moon (month) pass over us with blessings, Iman, safety, and in the belief of Islam. Grant us the ability to act on the actions that You love and Pleases You. (O moon) My Lord and Your Lord is Allah".

Dua upon breaking the fast:

ذَهَبَ الظَّمَأُ ، وَابْتَلَّتِ الْعُرُوقُ ، وَثَبَتَ الْأَجْرُ إِنْ شَاءَ اللهُ

Dhahab-az-zama'u, wabtallat-il-'urooqu, wa thabat-al-ajru in shaa'allaah

The thirst has gone and the veins are moist, and reward is assured, if Allah wills.

Dua During Ramadan: (Lailatul Qadr)

اللّهُمَّ إِنَّكَ عَفُوٌّ تُحِبُّ الْعَفْوَ فَاعْفُ عَنِّي

Allahumma innaka `afuwwun tuhibbul `afwa fa`fu `annee

O Allah, You are pardoning and You love to pardon, so pardon me.

23

DUA FOR PROTECTION AGAINST THE TORMENT OF THE GRAVE, HELL-FIRE & DAJJAL

اللَّهُمَّ إِنِّي أَعُوذُ بِكَ مِنْ عَذَابِ الْقَبْرِ، وَمِنْ عَذَابِ جَهَنَّمَ، وَمِنْ فِتْنَةِ الْمَحْيَا وَالْمَمَاتِ، وَمِنْ شَرِّ فِتْنَةِ الْمَسِيحِ الدَّجَّالِ

Allaahumma 'innee a'oothu bika min 'ad-haabil-qabri, wa min 'adhaabi Jahannama, wa min fitnatil-Mahyaa wal Mamaati, wa min sharri Fitnatil-Maseehid-Dajjal

O Allah, I take refuge in You from the punishment of the grave, from the torment of the Fire, from the trials and tribulations of life and death and from the evil affliction of Al-Maseeh Ad-Dajjal

Dua seeking good in this world and in the hereafter

رَبَّنَآ ءَاتِنَا فِى ٱلدُّنْيَا حَسَنَةً وَفِى ٱلْأَخِرَةِ حَسَنَةً وَقِنَا عَذَابَ ٱلنَّارِ

Rabbanaaa aatinaa fid-dunyaa ḥasanatan wa fil-aakhi-rati ḥasanatan wa qinaa ʿadhaab-an-naar

"Our Lord! Give us in this world that which is good and in the Hereafter that which is good, and save us from the torment of the Hell Fire!"

Dua To Fulfill All The Needs

لَّآ إِلَهَ إِلَّآ أَنتَ سُبْحَنَكَ إِنِّى كُنتُ مِنَ ٱلظَّلِمِينَ

la ilaha illa anta subhanaka inni kuntu minaz-zalimin

There is no deity except You; exalted are You. Indeed, I have been of the wrongdo-ers.

25

Printed in Great Britain
by Amazon

39004957R00016